pH Neutral History

Books by Lidija Dimkovska

POETRY

pH Neutral History

pH neutralna za životot i smrtta (pH neutral for life and death)

Anständiges Mädchen (Decent girl)

Idealna težina (Ideal weight)

Do Not Awaken Them with Hammers

Nobel protiv Nobel (Nobel vs. Nobel)

Meta-spânzurare de meta-tei (Meta-hanging on meta-lime)

Izgrizani nokti (Bitten nails)

Ognot na bukvite (The fire of letters)

Rožbi od Istok (The offspring of the est)

PROSE

Skriena kamera (Hidden camera), a novel

ANTHOLOGY (EDITOR)

20.mladi.m@k.poeti.oo (20.young.m@c.poets.oo)

Lidija Dimkovska

pH Neutral History

Translated from the Macedonian
by Ljubica Arsovska and Peggy Reid

 Copper Canyon Press
Port Townsend, Washington

Printed in the United States of America

Cover art: Kristina Bozurska, *Self-Portrait*

Author photo: Gerhard Gross

Copper Canyon Press is in residence at Fort Worden State Park in Port Townsend, Washington, under the auspices of Centrum. Centrum is a gathering place for artists and creative thinkers from around the world, students of all ages and backgrounds, and audiences seeking extraordinary cultural enrichment.

LIBRARY OF CONGRESS CATALOGING-IN-PUBLICATION DATA

Dimkovska, Lidija, 1971–
[pH neutralna za životot i smrtta. English]
pH neutral history / Lidija Dimkovska ; translated from the Macedonian by Ljubica Arsovska and Peggy Reid.
    p. cm.
Poems
ISBN 978-1-55659-375-8 (pbk. : alk. paper)
1. Dimkovska, Lidija, 1971– Translations into English.   I. Arsovska, Ljubica, 1950–
II. Reid, Peggy, 1939–   III. Title.
PG1196.14.I426P4213 2012
891.8´191 — dc23

                                                          2011044017

9 8 7 6 5 4 3 2   FIRST PRINTING

Copper Canyon Press
Post Office Box 271
Port Townsend, Washington 98368

www.coppercanyonpress.org

ACKNOWLEDGMENTS

The majority of the poems in this collection were originally published in Macedonian in *Nobel vs. Nobel* (2001, Blesok, Skopje) and *pH Neutral for Life and Death* (2009, Blesok, Skopje).

Grateful acknowledgment is due the editors of the following magazines, in which these poems first appeared in English:

American Poetry Review: "Ars Poetica Ballad," "Difference," "Projection," "Recognition 8," "Recognition 9"

The Café Review: "Called Back"

Common Knowledge: "Recognition 2"

Hayden's Ferry Review: "Recognition 3," "Recognition 4"

Verse: "Ballad for the Cesarean of Life," "Care," "Ideal Weight," "Is There a Better Wellness Than Death?," "Key," "The Living and the Dead," "Longitude," "Memory," "Pure Water," "Ripeness"

The Wolf: "Bonsai"

Words Without Borders: "Ballad of Aunt Else's Refugees"

Zoland Poetry: "Dental Poem in Golden Lane," "Recognition 5," "Recognition 6," "Recognition 7"

Contents

POEMS ABOUT LIFE AND DEATH

Memory   5

Bonsai   6

Difference   8

National Soul   10

Called Back   12

The Living and the Dead   14

Ripeness   16

Pure Water   18

Ideal Weight   20

Key   22

Is There a Better Wellness Than Death?   23

Care   26

Projection   27

Dental Poem in Golden Lane   29

Mustard   31

Longitude   33

My Grave   34

November in Graz   35

Correspondence with the World   37

RECOGNITION

1   41

2   42

3   43

4   *44*

5   *45*

6   *47*

7   *49*

8   *51*

9   *53*

BALLADS ABOUT LIFE AND DEATH

Ballad of Aunt Else's Refugees   *57*

Ballad for the Cesarean of Life   *64*

Ars Poetica Ballad   *69*

About the Author   *75*

pH Neutral History

Poems about Life and Death

Memory

My memory is a soldier's tin of bully beef
with no best-before date. I return to places
I have trodden with only one tongue in my mouth
and beat egg yolks for the natives to give them a good voice.
In the snow of the whites Jesus lies crucified as if in jest.
It takes two tongues for a French kiss,
now that I have several I'm no longer a woman but a dragon.
Like Saint George, I never learned
to give mouth-to-mouth resuscitation; my nose being blocked for years
I myself only breathe through others' nostrils, the world's paying.
"Aha! There's something fishy about you, something's fishy here,"
the little fallen angels
collecting old paper and plastic cry after me.
I love them best when they take their cots
out into the corridor to air the DNA away,
then A. and I sprawl out on them, a side each,
and in a carefully worked-out act of love
all our porcelain teeth chip off,
our gums turn into wide-open eyes, before which
our tongues in the darkness trip each other up,
growling, whimpering and moaning, and we
feel neither fear nor sorrow.
My memory is the black box from a crashed warplane
with no sell-by date. I return to places I have trodden
with only one blood under my skin,
I cross off fertile days for the natives on the calendars
with their name days and family feasts,
tame animals long for the wild, the wild for the tame.
Like a Jewish couple during fasts and monthly periods,
so God and I have been sleeping in separate beds for years.

Bonsai

Death horrifies the relatives abroad.
There's a plane to be caught, a walnut cake that'll give me ulcers
to be swallowed, a tongue to be burned with hot coffee,
and for lack of a farewell letter *Life* or the *Economist* to be read.
There are no articles for a section headed Culture in the Sundays.
Just articles on how to arrange your house, garden, paradise.
The telegram I sent travels with me,
but in business class. The man in the post office counted the words
        three times
as though they were an extinct species. Like a language that can
        be preserved
when there are just two women who don't know each other but gossip
        about the same man.
There are such women on my mother's side. The husband died yesterday.
And there are chairs at home I've never sat on,
with hard seats, reserved for the domestic saints
who come home only for funerals and weddings.
From now on we'll be giving each other relics as presents
on the anniversaries of the insurance policy
against damage caused by death.
The living charge for each death. With a small packet of paper
        handkerchiefs,
with new black knee-length stockings, with announcements on the
        LCD TV screen.
After the funeral I lie under the tree of life
like a bonsai waiting for the children of the dead one to play with it.
My veins shiver, my roots strain to hear the dead
who gurgle like little water heaters
and sprinkle hot water into my drop of dew.

It was so much easier when death was in God's hands,
when at nighttime I dried the river under the window with a hair dryer,
when the soldier bought me a carton of popcorn.
And now I even have a hobby: I go to commemoration services
for people I don't know. On the way back my stomach swells with all the
        fizzy drinks.
With speeches written double-spaced on the loss that's befallen us
here and now. We shall follow in his steps.
I drink blood-donors' blood and already I feel better. You should try it.
Put your life in order with the lottery ticket
and never cross out more than seven numbers. Because you too
have been tickled as a baby:
"I'll eat you up, I'll eat you up. . ." Love is the natural state
of cannibals. The others lie around on leather sofas
and bet on the last five minutes of Jesus's glory.
Will he be born, will he die, or be resurrected?
Messages will keep coming on the dead one's e-mail,
offers will keep piling up,
"Lose 5 kilos in 7 days, no charge."
And the tree of life will keep shrinking, the meat will keep diminishing
around the bone until it vitiates
the five meals a day, until it becomes a bonsai.
The only border between there and here is the plane's small window.
There I'm a tree for the timber industry, here I'm a little tree
        for meditation.
Life as usual mocks relatives abroad.
One must endure the flight, buy "travel fit" perfumes,
shut oneself up in the loo and pee for a long, long time,
until down there, on the grave, my bonsai becomes a tree with a shadow,
and then, in the absence of a will, read the *Financial* or the *Sunday Times*.
On Sundays there is no section headed Life.
Just articles on how to arrange your subconscious, your ego, your hell.

Difference

Jesusologists, Allahologists,
Constantinople has no contemporaries.
Everything here is professional,
toilet paper, washing machine,
the lift, the mike, the body mass.
Behind the perfection, the mind is a safe broken open
that hides nothing now but grief.
I live by a temple blotched with air conditioners
like grown-ups with belated measles.
Someone is asking me all day over the intercom
if there's an accordionist in the building.
The keeper of the flags might know —
one a black flag, tattered by domestic pets,
fluttering from suicides' balconies,
the other the national flag, faded with all the washing,
fluttering from murderers' windows.
Between birth and death life has no guarantee,
the only service station being the one still within ourselves.
Sometimes I burn with desire to be a war invalid,
to lie on a beach towel printed with a naked woman,
newly arrived from Sweden with the Red Cross.
But to no avail, for a day like this has need of my whole body,
and the night of my chest alone. No matter which hand I cross myself with,
the four sides of the world
miss the heart.
I'll protect it with a print on my T-shirt
of Che Guevara's head, or religious messages:
Taoism: *Shit happens.*
Buddhism: *It's only an illusion of shit happening.*

Islam: *If shit happens, it is the will of Allah.*
Jehovah's Witnesses: *Knock, knock: Shit happens.*
Christianity: *Love your shit as yourself.*
There's only one tune I can play on the accordion,
and even that is a remake of history.
I've sent the swab from my sick rabbit to Vienna,
and that from the sick saint — to Rome.
Just like Ingeborg Bachmann, each spare part
comes home in someone else's vehicle.
Existence lying supine in a hearse
that the living on the other side of the glass
take their hats off to
and wave as when he was born: *Bye-bye.*
When the beloved returned from Constantinople bearing the yellow quinces,
Fatima smiled at him sourly from the other world.
The difference between man and God, my darling, is just one:
Man first finds, then loses,
God first loses, then finds.

National Soul

Since my brother hanged himself with the telephone wire
I can talk to him for hours on the phone.
It is set constantly at *voice on*
so that his hands are free to stick
posters on God's poles
and call for a bitter debate on the subject:
Is the soul national?
Excitedly, we both tremble, do research,
me in this world, he in that.
Science has proved that the Russian soul, for example, is no more,
that in death those who dream of angels step on them as if they
      were shadows.
A Turkish soul might exist, my brother's voice crackles into the receiver,
since he hears the chirrup of Nazim Hikmet's kettle every morning
before he pushes the barrow of sesame rings
to the gates of Earth. I'll buy you one in memory of my dead ones.
And then he lapses into gasping silence. And we look for the
      Macedonian soul
among the number-plates on God's East-West highway,
in cardboard boxes labeled "Do not open! Genes!"
loaded on the backs of the transparent dead.
But one cannot rely on the dead.
The dead are illegal immigrants,
their swollen organs penetrating other peoples' lands,
with the jagged tips of their bones through their opening pits
they dig their final grave.
There they provoke their last fight too
for their national heavens
and for the soul that no one possesses any longer.

The number of the soulless grows, of the souls with no name to them.
They don't offer each other a seat on the bus; the ones and the others
        travel far,
then they search for each other through agents but don't meet up.
Nations throw insults at each other.
My brother despairs. I become A.-national.
The phone wire that connects us
slides out of my sweaty hand,
pinning the phone to the wall, retreating into the socket.
Why was no SOS line ever opened
for the unhappy ones in the other world?
Why did I never learn how to stop someone on the path to death?
I too, like my brother, have been splitting hairs since birth,
revelation at any price, unmask the meaning.
And the souls of those who split hairs
end up three ways: hanged with a telephone wire,
in the body of a poet, or both.

Called Back

You called me back and I had to return.
On the Peter Pan bus from New York to Amherst
with fifty cents change clutched in my left hand
and on leaving I fed it not into a coffee machine
but into your past to open the present.
And the present is a wolf with its belly ripped open
and filled with stones by the survivors,
not a drop of blood remains from it,
the victims have sucked it up while gasping inside,
hence their bitterness
in throwing it so cruelly into the river.
And the past hurts it, but it has nowhere to hide,
while it was different for you:
when you hid in your room
you hid in your time.
In the house with loaves of bread that never went hard
the saltcellar was the dial of death,
roots of black flowers pushed through the smallest holes,
and through the larger ones the whiteness of a dress as sharp as winter,
and through the biggest you yourself poured out:
"Is my Verse alive?"
Then death became an honored guest in the home,
sprawled for years in white stockings in the midst of the black bed linen
lying in wait for you should you cross the threshold of your father's house.
Your verse is alive, but I don't know if I am alive
as I stand once more in your garden in Amherst
reading the ad about exorcising zombies from poetesses' bodies
and wondering whether consciousness freezes at minus seven degrees
and how to sterilize the sterilizer

so that life will be life, and verse — verse.
Our meeting is like a rooster killed in honor of a guest from afar
writhing in the sunbaked dish of Amherst,
every bride's dress remembers your virginal one,
every bride's bouquet thrown over the shoulder wants to fall into
      your hands.
And what was left? A room — the first "Paper Only" dustbin,
uncertain for years as to whether it would end up in the dump
or with a secret reader in a rented room.
I did all I could for you. I have a husband, a daughter,
four eyes, two countries and two skies.
I came twice, but your house was locked.
So then I ran to the graveyard where at night you sit with Dara and Jim
on the fence, as if swinging above the earth.
There, to the right of the path strewn with blades of green grass
the Dickinson graves are lined up
like chemists' bottles,
but only yours bears the label
"Called Back."

The Living and the Dead

My nose always itches when I get to the graveyard.
The dead are docile at last, but not those
who bear their names. The heirs will first
rummage through the boxes with the deeds and dried flowers,
and only then drink sugared water and open the windows.
How come this money's no longer valid?
The wailers are served throat pastilles with their coffee.
My right arm itches too, but the candles brought from town
won't burn unless we cradle them.
In every house with a grandmother a child on holiday
restores the calendar saints with drops of wax;
in every house with a grandfather
eggshells are placed on the family album.
Not one man of my people is registered at my address.
Even though in childhood I had my hair cut at the barber's
and could ask any man in the street for the comb in his pocket
when all around me aunties were opening their sets of combs and mirrors.
Some never caught lice, others had their heads shaved.
The priest has introduced bleaching of the hair of prodigal sons,
before he cuts off a lock at their baptism. For a few days we all sent money
to the single mother with five epileptic kids,
but when she came out to thank us we couldn't but cry out:
"Were we collecting for you to dye your hair?"
The children all had a fit at the same time, kicking in slow motion
around their mother with Wella Flame Red on her hair. There was only
        hot tap water
at the hip-hop parties. I had to drink the hydrogen peroxide. To rinse out
the dead, who need a boost like beginners on their first school day:
"You have a lifetime to learn all you need to know."

A lifetime. In death, time is a bag with sports gear for gym.
And soon there will not be a single child without a Keep Dry T-shirt
and Keep Fast sneakers.
And soon there will not be a single corpse that won't be mine.

Ripeness

How could the lightning forever mist up the bathroom mirror
before it struck the one it was not supposed to?
So much trust in the thermometer behind the door,
so much suspicion of the national TV,
and when the boiler blew up in bits
the plumber was at a public celebration,
the presenter's stomach rumbled through one of the loudspeakers
and the fireworks caused a yo-yo effect in the other,
and when the pregnant women got back home
they could no longer fit into any shower cabinet.
Flood is the ripeness of drought
as death is the ripeness of life.
At night I go to bed with pads on my knees and elbows
lest I give in to the sweeping waters,
the color of dreams depends on the exchange of matter,
I stroke the traces of tomorrow with a spiky ball.
Was it in vain that I ceremonially laid my dental plaque
as the foundation stone of the museum cloakroom?
Hanging in it are the little coats that let Shakespeare's tempest through.
Before becoming A.-national I too used to pull on my life vest
over my head, but now I do it over my crash helmet.
My body is an exchange office in the Skopje Old Bazaar,
in front of it a heavy man with tattooed muscles and no umbrella
who won't let me in to get a receipt,
and with the money I exchange with him for a dreamless sleep
buys the spiritual leaders shoes made of devil's skin.
Some hold their Masses in them, others save them for appearances on TV,
we all have wet feet as if Mary Magdalene had washed them for us.
This morning again the chalice held only anemic plasma,

the babies sucked fingers dipped in distilled water

for batteries and irons, A.'s heart is now a cherry in jam,

now a morello in brandy. When I don't talk to myself for more than
    three hours,

the world becomes a cocktail on a bamboo rocker in the middle of a
    paying beach,

and after a few sips the sea cannot be seen, the sea cannot be seen.

Pure Water

On the same podium the poet from abroad reads and reads
and I keep sipping the water from his glass,
it's tasty, fresh and free of the layers of the centuries,
good both for a discreet gargle and for renewing the cells.
The audience looks at me reproachfully; from the front row
a woman in a blue costume shakes her fist at me,
and all but screams when I pour more water from the jug;
the poet calmly reads on, I lick my lips,
my kidneys overflow one into the other
like linden flowers into teacups;
he was obviously given a different glass from mine,
with a bottom of gray tinplate engraved with little black crosses,
like the empty tin hung above the village drinking fountain
by some visitor from the town, a crossword fan.
The poet reads with his nails dug into the corners of the lectern
and I hold my breath to swallow
the last drop of bioenergetic water —
if he carries on like this his hair will curl into a bun
and my wig will soar up without me into the sky.
At our side the past begins to growl like a wounded puppy
being pulled apart by its first cousins.
With a glass like this I could easily turn into sterile gauze
and sprawl under the collective memory in the missionary position,
and while the poet is slyly eyeing my ordinary glass
I can strain my own life, separate the pure water.
"Mine too," he whispers in a husky voice, and I squeeze
the little glass-cutter in my pocket and the test tube for spit smear,
and the culture shock makes the jug crack in front of our eyes.
The lectern is a red cistern with a hole in the pipe,

the audience jumps and tramples over us as if we were a barricade;
our broken bones transpire thermal water
that we drink in cupped hands, arms locked
in a trial of strength, but neither is stronger.
"Clean up after your guest," he screams with his last gasp.
"Clean up after your host," I beg him, drained.
"Clean up after your dog," he growls in his death throes.
"Clean up after your God," I silently answer, dead.

Ideal Weight

The middle class is body art on a family outing:
sprinkling their body and blanket hairs
with iron filings and lying there
depilating them with a magnet for the last time.
There are no biogarbage bins in purgatory. Leave me
your organs to be my aromatic sponges and compresses for my head
as I wade through the river of hydrochloric acid.
On the bank the intellectuals chant: "Design or die!"
but in vain—God at the side of a man who hasn't called on him
      since childhood
is like a knife at the side of a plate of spaghetti. He wears a bib
instead of a bathing costume.
Moscow's got her period, Philadelphia is one-ply toilet paper.
You know it yourself: in moments of historic decision
what is most fragile in one's life will crack: the kitchen chopping board.
It is then that the blade breaks from the razor,
and the Son from the Holy Mother.
When you enter the room, your cheek bleeding, I know you've seen in
      the mirror
the face of the baby that now weighs 370 g and is 21 cm long.
Like *Poly* salami, you say, and then we fall asleep on our feet.
The bear from the zoo snores hibernating in our freezer.
At night you cool your drink between its knees,
and between mine I squeeze the radio, tuned to longwave:
like a brick that's cooling down or a leaking hot-water bottle,
reality rocks in out-of-date news, every night I become ever more
      water-resistant.
Our river can be seen only through a small basement window.
And nobody dies absolutely anymore. The middle class scrapes

the price tags off presents, decorates windows with laser stars, plays
        shadow theater
with rubber gloves on. It makes faces at you as you cry:
"I exorcise zombies professionally! Be free again!"
and I know if you're too fat or too thin life and death are one and the
        same burden.
Only someone of ideal weight can carry the cross upright.

Key

When the key hung around your neck
your head was Buddha's tummy,
rubbed by relatives and entrepreneurs
with an unchanging New Year's wish
(money = health, happiness, and love),
they had their pet dream, you had your pet nightmare,
Bach on the radio, beans in the bowl, and Bruno Schulz
standing to attention in the shower cabinet.
A happy man gets charged up outside, and emptied at home
(pockets, stomach, brain, and sperm),
only the emptiness is left on the anatomical pillow
that remembers your head
even when the key has long since lost its string.
And now, when unhappiness too is a charging,
Buddha's tummy needs to be rubbed against the pillowcase
or be replaced by some newer deity,
changing the bed linen changes fortune too,
like a battery charger that no longer blinks.
You need a key for everything but your conscience
horticulturally arranged with an English lawn, a garden gnome, and a
          sensor fence,
a home where the one and only god is the community nurse
who comes to visit three days after the birth and three days before death.
In her black bag locked with a two-pronged key
once she carries scales to weigh life, the next time to weigh death.

Is There a Better Wellness Than Death?

Steiner came to tell us he was going to die.
We sliced cheese and salami,
poured three glasses of brandy,
the terrified children asked, "Before or after Christmas?"
He took out gold rings and chains from his pockets
and Swiss watches inherited from his granny,
gifts for many Christmases to come.
"Let my death not astonish you," he said,
and the children adorned with gold and watches
shook their heads in understanding.
"I slipped getting out of the thermal pool,
at 37°C every bone finds its right place,
and I left my hip in the chlorine footbath at the entrance
together with the locker key.
They made me lie down wearing my trunks in the ambulance,
my lungs jumping between the air conditioner's ribs,
the ambulance men played cards on my good hip,
at every bend my trunks swelled like a balloon.
In the hospital the doctor burst into tears unable to decide what was
        more important — the hip
or my lungs, why does this have to happen to me, he said,
a Gemini with Libra in the ascendant, that I have to decide
which death is better? So I lay for three days and three nights
in the corridor between the two wards,
and the doctor was tearing his hair out, plucking his eyebrows,
losing weight and consciousness unable to decide
which pain was more blessed,
the pneumonic one or the one caused by the fracture.
On the bank holiday I put an end to his suffering,

on my belly I asked for a one-way ticket for an ambulance
direct to the thermal pool,
the air conditioner blew my lungs up like feathers,
the attendants practiced somersaults over my good hip,
at every bend my trunks stuck to my skin,
the chlorine footbath in front of the pool was dry,
the locker in the changing room broken,
the pool gaped empty like a museum on a Monday.
I took the healthy organs from my body
and arranged them among the life belts,
it was time for the gray matter to relax,
and is there a better wellness center for the mind and body than death,
than that testamental message from my granny that, up there,
she'll rest, sleep well, and relax for ever and ever,
and I floated in bliss, and floating thus came to tell you
that I'm going to die, so you don't say afterwards that Steiner left suddenly,
don't slice any more salami and cheese,
don't bring more brandy. At the heavenly gates as well
they measure the cholesterol in the soul and use alcohol-tests
to see who's drunk on life so that he sinks legsdown,
while those who swim without any burden or memory
will reach Heaven, their legs held high, to God."
The children took advantage of the situation
and filled their mouths with cheese and salami,
while we were seeing Steiner off to the other world
they licked the brandy glasses too.
We watched the funeral several times on the Internet,
Steiner's grave was never found.
We exchanged the gold
for the latest technological games
and package arrangements to wellness centers.
Those who have no grave are happy and healthy in the other world too,
and we, wearing special shoes in the pool,

neither fall nor break hips, nor catch pneumonia,
only whenever we look at the watches
that Steiner inherited from his granny,
we see that time is flowing backward, feverishly,
the years are reduced to the moment we were born,
in three days in a row our children vanished
not to be found in any register of births or deaths,
and we are ever smaller, we forget that we exist,
just kick helplessly, and then succumb to the womb
with its massage jets, we roll under the mini-waterfalls
dragging us to the mouth of the uterus, dazed by bliss
we go blue in the pregnancy test, and then we're gone,
and this nonexistence is so light and good, and Steiner was wrong,
not death but nonexistence is the best wellness program.

Care

I wash the soup ladle as though I'm washing a baby's head,
with profound understanding I give it the complete treatment —
and I have been longing for a lice-destroying hair dryer
or a similar device against foreign bodies in the head,
but the world was slow when humanity was in question,
and fast when I stood at crossroads moving neither forward nor backward
and watched people and events of neither this nor that world.
I met ancestors I knew were long dead
in front of our door today,
they slipped away between the colors of the hedge
and I don't know if they continued in living or dead form,
but inside you were waiting for me, greeting me with a green bottle in
          your hand:
"It'll really come in handy, the shampoo our guests forgot!"
For a whole month we've been washing our hair with homemade
          olive extract,
strained and refined in some unidentified cellar,
and sometimes we abhor our selfishness
so we subject other semiliving entities
to moderate shampooing:
I wash the head of the porcelain angel (bearing a pottery mark)
and he wriggles between my fingers like a captured moment;
you rub the mane of the wooden horse (on a pedestal)
and it leaps in your hand like a court jester at a ball.
We were all spoiled by the shampoo the guests forgot,
but we don't know if it's been patented for the care or the removal
of jinxes, alien thoughts, and dandruff from parallel worlds.

Projection

Laurie Anderson had a bad night.
Her bare arms gave the impression of cul-de-sacs in the dark.
The muscles grieved for total darkness.
Darkness, said Laurie, is the projection of the core
which although invisible is the goal of the electronic erection.
Laurie, I believe you met God face-to-face.
I met him face to face to face. Nobody knew who was addressing whom.
The people were turning to look at the blond in silk stockings,
the blond was turning to look at the nun with her head down.
Everyone thinks that in border situations like this
God looks at the one in black robes. But you, Laurie, know
that he looks at the one looking at the nun
and it's on her silk stockings that he sticks the "God's child" label.
God knows if he also pinches her as well.
But, that's their business. I look at my hands
attacked by love staphylococci.
I'm freezing in my folk-embroidered blouse
because she too was crazy about Indian blouses.
And he was crazy about Levi's
but may darkness swallow me up if I tell him that.
Sweet prohibition, keep Laurie's hands in good shape!
The contents of the bag are emptied into hot water,
boiled for thirteen minutes and served with cream.
Then Laurie's aunt tells her Andersen's fairy tales.
Then Laurie's aunt dies
and the old maid is buried in a wedding gown.
Laurie interrupts the priest and sings to her aunt:
In the world beyond, a husband is waiting for you,
that's where you'll find your happiness.

You're a bitch, Laurie, and a big one at that!
But I know that you know how your palms itch when you're alone,
when the electricity goes off,
and the silence whirls in your stomach.
I know that you know how hard it is
to dress in white after wearing black,
to have your arms not merge into the day
but be signs by the road,
and to have nobody, Laurie, nobody travel
down your roads.

Dental Poem in Golden Lane

On leaving Golden Lane
the men took out their sharp-toothed pocket combs
and briskly smoothed their reflexes
—silver-white like K.'s visions,
the women tied their sizzling heads in deer-hide scarves
—payments in-kind instead of their monthly salary for May,
and I repeated the exercises for a thin neck
clutched in plaster as if in the arms of someone drowning.
In that small house no. 22 the guide stabs his cry at us:
"I'll get myself gold teeth, porcelain alienates me!"
We step with tight lips, the world is a vacuum denture,
the echo of the voice resounds in different languages,
but the ascent wants tongues hanging out, not an installation
of pocket combs, hides, and a plaster-wrapped straw.
At night the street is locked
with a golden key, lest K. wake as a tourist.
And maybe the mouth full of precious beads
will no longer chatter idly about the gravity underfoot,
but will be as light as a saltcellar tipped over,
or the anatomical insole of a bride's shoe?
Don't ask me, K. I clean my teeth every night with A.'s visiting cards,
I plasticize my breath and between my gums,
I stratify my own closeness as if in a gutter.
And my neck is made of plaster to prevent my mind from shriveling,
and my combs are behind my ears so that the rescuer will hear me.
I am not even my own guide through the rooms of the absurd,
that's why neither gold nor porcelain can harm
the enamel of my wisdom tooth. Only these white visiting cards

with black codes in Golden Lane
pick again and again at K.'s decision:
"Fillings neutralize me, I'll get myself milk teeth."

Mustard

We ran out of mustard at home, and on Sunday afternoon
even the neighbors won't answer the door,
the children being with their unmarried aunt,
and the neighbors move their love from the corner to the attic,
from the attic to the bathtub,
and without mustard the frankfurters are homosexuals
caressing only from nine to nine thirty
when the policemen have hot dogs and french fries,
and at that very time we ran out of mustard,
we looked each other in the eye: who's going to condemn whose greed?
We have said mustard is for Sundays only
when everyone else is making soups and apple pies
and roasting chicken, and you drew the curtains in all the rooms,
had me masked as a pirate-woman and mixed me rum
with carnelian cherry syrup, and "Come on, let's play
kidnapping starfish, ministars, and well-known stars of jazz.
Wait, you've got something in your eye, something we need
right now, before the frankfurters have cooled,
before their skin has slipped off them.
You see, my darling, your eyes are the color of mustard!"
And he left me no time even to laugh. With a little spoon
he took out my eyes, popped them into the empty mustard jar,
mixed them well, mincing them better than the kitchen Multipractic.
"Done," he said, "it's good the frankfurters haven't cooled off completely,
bon appétit"—and he dipped one in the mustard which, as if alive,
trembled around the frankfurter's head.
I was watching all this with my third eye.
I even reached for a frankfurter myself.
"Aha, so you'll have the biggest one!" "No, no, just. . ." "Yes, yes, you
        always just. . ."

The mustard had yellowed his teeth.
"God, I cried, are you all right?" And he went on chewing
and dipping in the mustard, nodding his head:
"Wonderful! The mustard is first-class!"
I simply watched him, trying to stop him in my mind,
but it was all in vain, he yellowed through and through,
like mustard in a factory mold,
I covered him with my third eye and even said happily to myself:
"It's good he gulped the frankfurters in time,
for there he is, all that's left of him is mustard
that's passed its use-by date,"
and one thought bit into my third temple.
"It's good we didn't make the french fries.
Or he'd've taken this eye as well to make a ketchup!"
The TV was showing a documentary on health food.

Longitude

A., measure the longitude from the premature death
to the resurrection at an inopportune time (at five p.m.)
when even God naps with his mouth open so that I have
to call my grandmother, bewitched in reality,
to get me used to the angles of life again,
to the sharp edges of the cardboard cutouts,
color in with crayons the longitude between the ordeals
that I wear on my head instead of hair dye,
like a basket of cereals or slaughtered chicken,
like the dowry of a systematically examined granddaughter.
How long can it be, a longitude
between hands that save themselves for a wise decision?
I would like to bite God to pus,
just as I bite my nails, to be older than him,
and to watch him grow and become addicted to me,
and then I myself covertly put powder in his five o'clock tea
to break the addiction as I overtly put in your heart
addiction drops, and I spray the cat
on the windowsill for enlightenment.
The changing of the guard before the royal palace
is a modern dance of the old senses, consumer fever,
a Longitude between the post-mortals and immortals,
stretcher and stretcher-bearer, a three-year visa in a golden frame,
so that I can pawn it in the bad pre-European times,
a hyphen between your sign and my symbols.
A.-national, A.-political, A.-social Longitude
— zero mm from life to poetics.

My Grave

Every day I watch my grave in the yard
included in the price of the house,
with a board over the hole,
with a tombstone of white limestone,
with a photograph in a gold frame,
and the year of birth separated by a dash
from the empty space for death.
The grave is there under the pear tree facing the house
staring at me even when I have my back turned to it.
In spring the cats loosen the board,
and sparrows in the tree shit on it for good luck,
in summer an occasional overripe pear
chips off a piece of the tombstone,
in autumn the rain thins its spine, bites its figure,
in winter the snow rams it deeper into the ground.
It's the focal point of every thunderbolt,
of every earthquake — it's the epicenter.
It crumbles, decays, decomposes,
it's becoming ever smaller, more wizened, brought to its knees,
the grave is disappearing before my eyes,
it's falling into its own hole, turning from dust to dust.
I look at it this morning, what's left of it is no more
than a small pile of limestone being scattered by the wind,
broken shards of board big enough to build nesting boxes,
and the photo in its gold frame
flutters around the from–to dash.
My grave is vanishing faster and faster,
just like my life.

November in Graz

To survive November in Graz
when the mirrors in public toilets
are misted with the breath of political refugees,
when vacuum cleaners moan
like dictators in their typists' bedrooms,
when my bathrobe is a frozen flag on the fortress,
to survive November in Graz
with a Cuban family in exile on the floor below,
to cover your ears and in an attack of powerlessness
snatch the wastebin from the hands of the woman
who won't let go while her husband weeps and the child is kicking him,
and to read Hannah Arendt behind seven doors, hugging the heater.

To survive November in Graz
when life has gone to some other place,
sits in the empty amphitheater, rummaging through the thorns,
while my ancestors' remains are no longer there,
it's only my brain that's still archaic, my body is of the present;
we always stain our honor ourselves,
and our hands are always stained by someone else.
Bent over the railing at the Schloßberg
I follow with the probe of my eye three shadows on the floor below,
and want to be the woman embroidering on a frame in the fortress lift
on a stool upholstered with the skin of the man she caresses when
     she's alone,
and mother of seven daughters she lovingly calls sonnies.

To survive November in Graz
with the carnivorous plant branching in the bathtub

when a rainbow appears on the bottom of the pot
and church bells break the sound barrier of the fortress —
time is a marathon runner, and I'm not in any shape at all,
bound without wires to the posthumous remains of the city
I'm asking myself whether life will know how to return,
to find the way and energetically ring the upper bell,
to surprise me staring at my Cubans without Cuba in the news
and reinhabit bones, existence,
or whether every future November
in Graz I will have to survive, dead.

Correspondence with the World

to E.D.

Three drawers contain my entire correspondence with the world:
in the first — empty envelopes and stamps no longer valid
to the world I have never written to;
in the second — small self-addressed stamped envelopes
from the world that has written to me at my expense;
in the third — dust caught in spider's webs:
the only trace of the world that has never answered my letters.
And now, seated on the small chipboard chest,
as my ears burn I realize:
but of course I too am someone's conscience,
someone's first and last love,
someone must be talking about me,
and as others are in my dream I am in someone else's,
a prayer, a swearword, or a curse.
Many deaths are linked through my life,
I was an old child with wrinkles
and everything was clear to me, yet I understood nothing.
And now, when I myself have become a letter?
Not the full face but the profile is the essence, the self, the fate:
an ear, an eye, a nostril, a palm, a heel,
a kidney, lung, breast, ventricle.
There is no dialogue between couples, doubles,
the twenty-first century has alienated them. Individual men,
      individual women,
it's always their individual way even when the world
is one and only. There's no such post office where letters can be sent
that won't come back. Every correspondence
is an autopsy of thought.

World, you to whom I've written, who've written back to me or not,
    you knew:
I have never wanted to get far,
but close,
as close as possible
to the most distant.

Recognition

to A.

1*

On May 22 the sky's bile burst.
I bit my nails with succulent delight
and now myths drip on me:
they are a summer dress on the clothesline.
Ammonia will leak out, gurgle, gurgle.
The hems will dry quickly, quickly.
A. asks whether Medea is in verse.
I am all bruises
and I know why the sky is kitsch today
like a reproduction of Da Vinci
on a packet of stockings.
Better look at my undeveloped eyes, A.,
'cause today I'm yours, today, today
when the twenty-second day is not an expression
of internal unity, A. But it's us, A.
I saw a bride without a groom in my dream
on a city bus, click!
She shouldn't marry, she shouldn't.
This morning Tsvetaeva cries out.
You all, I say, can't get used to me
being the dark side of fate?!
A., look into my undeveloped eyes, A.
The sky is as it's always been, and time
doesn't whistle echoes, I am the one here
who inhales. That's the way it is with her!
You love Her, she loves You AND that's all She wants.

*The first poem in this section is translated by Ilija Čašule and Thomas Shapcott.

2

I'd say I'm a period baldachin on a bed,
I'd say you're the key to a hermeneutic poem.
And am I not, am I not only
a miniature sculpture by Brancusi
in the Pompidou Centre, Paris,
which nobody notices, after all those paintings,
more exhausted by the cameras of the Asians, Scandinavians,
and even some of our people,
am I not yours there more than anywhere else,
especially since I've seen you there with the other woman,
especially since I've seen you there when I was alone, entirely alone.
Then I was jumping two or three steps at a time
all the way to the cellar where *L'amour, c'est le pop art,*
yes, Brancusi in the center of Paris
lived in a typically Romanian room,
and I, on the periphery of Little Paris,
live in your truth.
Am I handsome, you're asking me, am I handsome?
My eyes are not to be trusted
even though you bought me deerskin
to wipe my pupils clean,
but the amorous look with which I followed you
from my little bronze forms
says you're the handsomest,
especially when you open the old wound,
especially when you place love and art on the same level
and cry because of that,
a little out of happiness, a little out of sorrow.

3

Relatives pull. Unknown people pull.
Detergent advertisements pull,
and the Byzantine churches pull to Vespers.
Tzvetan Todorov's alienated man pulls me by the sleeve
as I pull my roots upward.
The rosary is in my pocket. Jesus's years
are as beautiful as your hips,
my contemporary man.
The town sweepers' wrinkles pull.
The nuns' milky faces pull. My friends married and unhappy pull me by
       the hair,
I pull my unfound husbands by the nose.
May the patriarch's head be shaved!
May the president of the state let his hair grow!
I don't know how many have returned to Love,
but they pull, the wretched, the two poles pull
toward the so-called Truth.
I'm cold I'm hot I'm loved I'm not
I'm pulled by the hand: here, this is how I want
to be burnt when I die,
for you to keep me in a jar next to the night lamp.
I pull him by. . . And I, I want you
to bury me in a sixty-kilogram word.
And an end to all bipolar dramas!

4

How can I have the name I have,
having missed classes in swimming in the River Lethe?
I could be nothing but a woman *in praesentia*
who this morning walked between two traffic lights
with one white and one black sandal on.
I'd say that I've finally become intertextual.
I could even be extratextual,
but my head is shaved, and you love me.
I sit on the edge of the balcony and think:
"Now, when Granny's dead,
shall I still write pastoral poetry?"
They are spraying against mosquitoes again.
Even under the bed although it does not know how to buzz,
just squeaks and falls from the seventh floor
together with the line of defense, the thesis,
the Chinese students' vowels,
and I fall, but naturally up, up,
toward the perfect floor, soft like Terra's clouds.
With you it's all upside down,
dreaming is vertical, Monday's a holiday,
and naturally — *in veritate vinum.*
As for me, that's a miracle indeed,
I was dead, and now am alive,
and as this existence flows in the opposite direction
and you love me, you love me more and more.
I know, I'm already immortal.
Ah, if only you could've loved my granny Vetka
that much!

5

People think that I'm crying.
And I simply wear inappropriate contact lenses
which scratch my eyes in self-observation.
The white of my eye is a map of roads crosscut with rails.
The train that brought you was long ago withdrawn from use.
Have you got sturdy legs for your return to the womb?
Or else a wheelchair?
I have no one to bless my home.
The priests' wives murmur. The dolls are impossible.
All night long they stand on their heads and curse
human values. God pretends to understand them.
But still, I'm not an abstract woman.
Had I been able to enter into you,
your metabolism would have been in order,
and I could have seen the world with eyes undamaged
by inappropriate literature in childhood.
The bells tolled solemnly and the rhythm flowed smoothly.
No, she shouted! My bells toll folk-style,
intermingling with the sound of Granny Vetka's bell,
Constantine! You're a constant spirit in the little dents along the walls
like these bugs crawling along my conscience.
I became an infanticide. Even the graves die.
His life is empty and the fridge is full.
When the angel flew away an earthquake shook happiness.
Don't cry, don't cry, or we'll call Uncle Freud!
No, it's just my lenses irritating the erotic spot.
And the child is not mine. You know whose it is?
It's... It's... It's... But, you finally fell asleep. Paris is always so close,
I have only to stretch my arm, but he's far away from the Seine.

Wash my eyes with you. Make a path for me, the half-blind woman, to Notre-Dame. Give me the Communion with a finger in my mouth. Recognize me, damn it, recognize me.

6

I was not beaten in a sack.
That's why I can't see you upside down,
and still less can I believe in cities
founded in postwar agreements on cultural cooperation.
The fallen hero asks me the time,
and the watch, I can see, has grown a small tummy.
Out of universal awareness I no longer shake hands
but only nod my head. This little body in my sleeve
is proud meat perfect for practical classes in anatomy
in the electronic hospital. I put on your shirt
and I hit my arm against teacher Slobodanka's memoirs.
Every experience is a bit immoral.
You'd better fill the sack with graffiti like this one:
"I'm a happy cube! (–16°C)"
You'd better turn me toward you in your inside pocket,
and I'll be repeating it to you, the folk message:
"Take your pocket knife, unstitch the lining,
that's where I've hidden the last sin."
But the sack's a good human invention for people like us.
Inside it we're finally three-dimensional,
and time was born just today. Had I known
that birth's brief and breathless
as an international phone call,
I would've been able to learn shorthand,
I would've been able to measure the chicken's pulse
as you're filling it with nuclear sky
like a kaleidoscope or a bathtub.
But would I have been able to fill the sack
with gnawed bones without saying to you:

Aleš, you know what? It was on the news
that the assassination attempt against the president
was the deed of no one else but Scheherazade!

7

I got up on my left foot and I stood like that
until the floor detached itself from black thoughts.
The foot feels a cramp. Thoughts are steps that have migrated
to a cannibal society. Then why do they
say I'm bodiless and a beast on top of that?
I was looking for myself in the glass door — it saw me.
A myopic look corrected by contact lenses,
the only form of body at the end of the century.
The neighbor called me to try on some imported dresses.
I locked myself in her bedroom
and tried on silicone eyes. I didn't know her husband kept them
in mothballs. They smelled of my memory.
If they are too loose, my mother will take them in for you.
And does your mother know how to let out
creatures made to the measure of imported dresses?
And just out of spite I stood on my head all afternoon
(luckily Balkan women don't suffer from headaches,
the headache, neuropsychiatrists would say,
is typical of independent women who have remained alone),
out of spite I made you memories, turned you out of the house,
reported you to the police. The police caught you,
beat you up. *If you're the head of the household, then you're the head —*
      they told you —
if not, you need a head. Next time you'd better not leave her on her own!
Now we have neither a floor nor a ceiling.
I live in a wall clock and all day long I cuckoo.
When you don't want to know the time
I become nervous and vulgar: I swear and spit.

And it's intolerable, it is, this ease of living,
but what, what do the clinically dead say,
what do they say of, God forgive, existence?

8

How dirty your feet are, A.,
I could plant basil in them,
and even rape could take root,
only, if possible, the pores of your skin beg me,
no sugars and no preservatives. Health food
for a healthy family, a condition stipulated in the virtual contract,
and nobody asked us if we have cockroaches at home,
and if we do, whether they are intellectuals, or
do they, too, like the still lifes in the garden,
serve as models for amateur painters.
Colors which hide in the ideas of them,
paranormal configurations,
and your feet, A., are so black
that even the plants in the school herbarium
would rise from the dead linked to their webpage.
Nothing will wash the medieval statues,
or the memories of the night in the underground
when the midget got under the model's dress
and she just glanced at her wristwatch,
took her *Elle* out of her handbag, and started reading
as if unaware of the body between her ideal measures,
well it was then, A., that history overturned like the swingboat
in the funfair, scattering hats,
civil wars, and public apologies —
everybody was staring at your feet of black marble
on the white map of fallen empires.
A priest said: Let me wash your feet brother,
but I just managed to show him
the birthmark on your right hip.

And this year again summer is the season when mosquitoes
infect the subconscious with malaria,
and I'd better plant some basil
in your black feet of natural proteins,
classified as environment-friendly with green apple,
only you seem to disapprove, you don't know what it's like to be a
        mobile garden,
and I'm saying to you, darling, even graves are mobile,
let alone a garden of basil roots
that sprouted first in my life, and in your feet
they just suck the power that does not know its power:
first it's a midget, then a model, then—history itself.

9

You have a sense of direction even in worlds
you've never visited, A.
You can tell what personal misery will give birth to a work of art
that will travel the world like the mind of an imbecile.
And which imbecile will return from no-man's land, and which won't.
That's why in Christian bookshops
you pause with the Bible open in your hands
to listen to the singer simulating orgasm on the radio.
An exchange of ideas, isn't it? Before she finishes, the monk
manages to find the cassette with chants performed by the monks of
    Mount Athos,
but the customers are already leaving. *Encore une fois.*
I must tell you that in East European countries
the best-looking men are the Mormons: the side-parting of their hair
radiates with first love, something in their gait
brings glamorous fashion shows to mind. Was it you who told me
the joke: "Do you know whose creations Lady Di is wearing now?"
"I don't know." "Versace's."
Mormons have muscles of spume.
They float above obscurantism in waves like
true Balkanophiles.
The only ones. I'm trying to tell you
that the retired teacher was caught selling drugs
in the neighborhood and together with her former students
the cobblestones slipped into the river during the night,
but you're not listening to me. Why did you repeat all night:
"Flambé. . . flambé. . . flambé. . ." Do you want us to go for a flambé?
The child. . . the child from the house that caught fire was burning in
    my hands,

while I was running to the hospital, but when I got there it was too late.
The doctor said: "Oh, it has turned flambé." Now I know how you get bulimia.
And only out of fear of breaking the glasses you bought me for my birthday
I poured the poison into a plastic pot
(my grandfather kept his cut-throat razor and brush in a pot just like
          this one),
but I felt the smell of decomposing beard, so I threw it into the sea.
It'll have a hard time decomposing for several centuries,
and I'll be vomiting in vain babies wrapped in eco-paper.
Don't sully it with letters, A., letters are out of fashion.
You'd better turn it into a nudists' beach.
Sociolinguistics of lunatics vowed to silence.

Ballads about Life and Death

Ballad of Aunt Else's Refugees

It's cold in Schloßberg. The stoves are full
of our nails and hair. The elevator with coal and matches
remained stuck in the middle of the hairdresser's by the city gate.
We had our forelocks trimmed for free there,
and now we look at each other as if in a mirror, pH neutral.
When Aunt Else adds knitting to our slippers
we play darts: she aiming her blue knitting needle
at our hearts, we our red at hers. *Grüß Gott.*
The Elastoplast stops the blood in the wound,
and accelerates the asylum procedure.
And love. It's going to be all right, Aunt Else says.
The first to tell us, "Come on, Europe doesn't eat people,"
encouraging us in a muffled voice, her breasts rising like a wet nurse's,
leaning against the wire netting on the mountain when breathless
we plunged our foreheads into the magic cubes of air
not knowing whether the flight had ended or just begun.
"There," she said, "the netting's broken here, and from here on
everything's going to be all right,
these are not handcuffs, these are only wristbands I have knitted myself."
Handmade, red seal of quality.
Wristband after wristband in her grip we became hers and she ours.
The border was no more than a varicose vein that could be hopped.
Like a skipping-rope, like a hopscotch square. . .
The carpet in Schloßberg has seven squares,
a stone for each continent and one for Aunt Else.
Life is a rehearsal for another life
that will not knock on weak students' doors.
So that no students fail the grade
Aunt Else kisses us on the forehead before we go to sleep,

and at night takes our arms out from under the covers
to place them as in the illustrations in a children's magazine.
Around the glasses with B complex
B_3 and B_6 tie our intestines into a Gordian knot.
In the morning, Aunt Else no longer has dandruff,
or we flat feet. We eat apple strudel.
That's how it has always been: to keep in shape it is necessary
to deceive time tossed into the sports bag behind the door.
We wave through the chimney at the children filing in
to classes in life experience.
"These, children, are refugees," the teacher says.
"And what do they take refuge from, teacher?"
From gravestone photographs.
Aunt Else carries a Smena camera round her neck.
In worn-out clothes we spread three drops of oil
or some sugar on slices of stale bread for the children (all paid for by
        the school).
The children eat and throw up and then suck squashed strawberry sweets
that all of us have hoarded in our sweat-suit pockets.
Thus modern children acquire memories,
and we do not forget about our origins.
Aunt Else takes their measurements too for wristbands.
In the teacher's black handbag with "Pink Bag" written on it
ground eggshells stay for forty days,
then she mixes them up with mayonnaise and ketchup
to use in calming the pupils giggling in the back row:
"The tram door nearly sliced Mum's head off yesterday,
so today she rode to work on the back of the Spanish mastiff."
Our mothers used to go to work wearing socks over their boots,
that's why we've come such a long way.
The city hangs above us like a shelf giving way under heavy dictionaries,
we take them one by one and put them on our heads
running between Herrengaße and Mura, refugees *in praesentia.*
Instead of watches we wear blood pressure gauges over our wristbands,

the tongue is a lift between love systoles and diastoles.
Already in childhood our feet have touched the bottom, and some
even the border. Sorrow is an orthopedic error, Aunt Else says.
And there, the city swimming pool calls us to therapy:
"Swim forty days as Jesus swam
in the eye of the Father, be fit and healthy,
water is the best massage for a refugee, that's how Jesus survived Golgotha,
spend your Christmas fast in a bathing suit,
relax, Jesus relaxed too when he walked on the water."
We look questioningly at Aunt Else, and she turns the hourglass.
It's time for the belly button to draw in, for the tongue to stick out,
for each of us to fill the union's New Year's gift bag
with washing powder and some ash.
Applications are ineptly written, washing machines are full,
but those who look will see and those who wash—will dangle on
        the clothesline.
All the days when we do not appear
in the newborns' dreams are holidays.
Then we call the street below the castle by a pet name
in honor of the people's hero's anniversary.
Aunt Else is glad. "You're just mine now," she says, "but—
little by little you'll become theirs too." And how many heroes
are there on the other side of the river? For each refugee a toe and a finger.
We visited the city maternity home. The big screen in the hall
shows an ad featuring a child crying and banging its head on the floor
for chocolate, and the father blushes with shame.
I told you, *use a condom.*
Two rows of concrete mixers—bellies twisting in a dance,
mothers-to-be ripening with their sons in incubators,
and girls are born with a maiden name.
And we are refugees, the flight's eternal—
from country, from the echo of the embryo in the hallway, from the
        heart's zigzag,
from the oxygen in the radiators. Aunt Else is giving wristbands

to the fathers stretched out on the delivery beds.
It feels nice when you cross your hands to make a seat.
We sit on them and wait for a reply.
The authorities are sending e-mails with red exclamation marks.
They want us to remain refugees, a vulnerable category that can
        be squeezed
through the eye of a needle, a new brand of microchip.
The journalists report we may, so we do, wear size XS,
but our files are clinical cases, fat XXL.
We'll solve the file problem. We'll send Aunt Else
to the church printing house, they'll thin our files out
printing them on Bible-weight paper. It takes an instant and life is holy.
This wait hasn't been so long after all.
And on Fridays Aunt Else gives her dentures a rest
and they sit alone in a plastic pot in the bathroom,
all the windows and doors are shut — a vacuum, she says,
makes both people and gadgets last longer —
we drink runny broth and tomato juice,
a spring cleaning of God's dust in us,
then sprawled on the floor we giggle quietly
because Aunt Else never leaves the house
for fear she might meet death
that every Friday slips through the *Kunsthalle* back entrance
and might easily sneak into our file.
Love is measured in square meters.
We are refugees, we know how to flee death,
but Aunt Else has no experience with cheating fate.
And we all use the papers in the files to make her trendy paper-chains
        of figures
in black-and-white designs, with a blue seal in the middle and a signature.
Like covering textbooks with pages from some old calendar —
twelve subjects, twelve months — and notebooks
with the cellophane left over from jars of winter preserves.

All the refugees in this world have both gender and memories.
We shall mate, we shall multiply, we shall divide.
Everyone has to be alone in a passport, even an unborn baby,
and only we are a list folded in Aunt Else's passport.
If you flee, when abroad you don't speak to strangers
about sex or politics, so the aunts on our mothers' side advised us.
For the first you'll be arrested, and killed for the second.
So nobody talks. And silence itself is both sex and politics.
Aunt Else spreads her arms like Medea
and won't give us up. "We are shut in
because I don't wear my dentures on Fridays,
but when you're shut in with equals, there's nobody to kill you."
Wise and sweet is Aunt Else as sweet boiled wheat.
You could live with her in exile as though in
a mountain lodge. The floor creaks when we are out—
the hearth gasps, the mountain turns into a plain.
On Fridays our very self gets sterilized.
But look, a wasp has just come through the broken glass
of the spy-hole in the door, buzzed dazzled around our heads,
astounded by our Lego identities
and disconcerted by the temperature differences between indoors
        and out—
stung Aunt Else on the neck, just above her bioenergetic necklace.
We had an attitude to death, but did not know what dying was
in a country where dying is a registered packet, and death
an electronic message, while it's an unsealed telegram where we
        come from.
And here is Aunt Else prostrate on our paper-chains and dying,
and we pair mended socks and cry, seeing the beads of the necklace
as pupils of eyes and magnifying glasses:
the blind regain their sight, but Aunt Else is not resurrected,
once a refugee always a refugee.
In the chapel the priests stretch their arms to God,

one-two-three-three, two-two-three-three,

morning exercise for firm muscles,

not even in prayer will spirit and body separate,

but we have to separate from Aunt Else.

"Was she meat-eating or vegetarian?" we were asked in the office,

but we could not remember. When she was the one she was not the other

and vice versa. "You are orphans now," the hostess said.

And closed the furnace with her little finger. The door caught our fingers.

We sucked them in our mouths.

The seals on our wristbands turned blue.

The crematorium is an eco-and-veggie system.

As if from a potter's wheel an urn of ashes emerges from it.

Who needs a coffin with a corpse in the bedroom?

Graves are meat-eating. In our countries the biggest of all.

Like a dog that's attached itself to the butcher's. Or to the city
        slaughterhouse.

It is only through inertia that the dead are packed in boxes, rather than

in paper or in a plastic bag. And the grave eats them, chews them,
        grinds them,

greedily, insatiably, clothes not buttoned. Throws odd bones

behind the chapel for luck. And then falls asleep, until the next supper.

And there are dead in this world and in that.

Aunt Else's body has warmed the stove in Schloßberg.

We shall burn her knitting wool in it on the last night.

The fire will crackle announcing visitors no one will welcome.

Tomorrow the authorities will resettle us across the asylum centers
        of Europe.

A refugee once is without escape forever.

And let us now eat rolls with salami and cheese,

like at the good old funerals in our native countries

(fathers we still have, but not fatherlands)

when boxes traveled on the local buses,

those holiday gifts for the dead's beloved.

Aunt Else must've sent some too. Without her our pain
spatters in the eyes of the priests like a pimple.
And never again will Aunt Else say:
"Let's start the week with a clean lavatory bowl."
With a clean mirror on which a breath is God's message.
These rolls are tasty, a compass in our fate.
To our left the cemetery of the meat-eaters, to the right that of the
       veggie dead—
you can easily slip through the middle and disappear,
but where can you go, what sea can you enter bearded
and come out smooth-skinned? How can you become
a banana seller on a beach, and what is more, how can you shout
"Vitamins for Sex Machine!" Sex and politics are things you don't
talk about in foreign countries. History is karaoke:
it repeats what life has learned from a book.
After the funeral everybody goes to the sale in a big store,
to change out of their mourning black,
only we shall slip naked into the big Thule trunk
on Aunt Else's minibus, we shall close the lid on ourselves,
grasp each other's wristbands, and like paper-chain figures
in a breeze by the open window we too shall fly
not up but down, through the telescope of our own blood,
of our shared freedom. Aunt Else, Aunt Else,
everyone else can flee, but not a refugee.

Ballad for the Cesarean of Life

At that time she was just a little girl weeping only over the butcher
who adorned with money and an apple in his mouth
is leaving on a lifelong honeymoon —
while her clockwork puppy
tears apart the elastic of her pajamas, but puts its tail
between its legs before the little bears. The little bears
defend the A.-sexual territory to this day.
When she takes a bath, her mother tells those phoning her
she's at the store so they won't imagine her naked.
And in the store nakedness is chewing gum given instead of change,
a slipper on the wrong foot. Dressing is crucial
to worldwide liberty. She tries on clothes in changing rooms
with her shoes on. There is no such thing as unsoiled liberty.
The next time tell them she's at the butcher's. That she's hanging on a hook
above the yellowed newspaper obituary for a bridegroom, bride, and driver.
The Rent-A-Car agent dashed to the mortuary to collect the debt,
and on his way out slipped bloody needles into her hand,
and instead of into an insectarium
she thrust them into her heart under her pajamas.
They only pricked her a little, just enough to make her run across the park,
before the national hero from the last war pinched her bottom.
Every winter she comes back again and again
with a red-hot rod to her Snowman in the yard
to pierce his heart while taking care
not to scorch her coat that's not easy to inherit.
At night she won't light the fire until her bladder becomes a political organ
demanding a special TV channel, birthday candle, and
butterfly-stroke swimming. The temperature of the urine
is ideal for a baby's bath. On Lexington Avenue

the diarrhea that she'd smuggled in from Djerba
ran down into the shoes of unmarried Misters Universe.
The maid in the hotel watered her for three days,
but she didn't bloom. The electrolytes flew over the avenue
and spattered on the YUSA Corporation's window in the building opposite.
The cleaning lady pulled the chair from under the sleeping boss,
ran to the underground and at the last stop
her heart burst with laughter, and the boss, legs up like a cockroach,
dreamt all night of baby's excrement.
She too had once pulled the chair from under her mother
to sit by the stove and watch over the green-handled knife
that the neighbor opposite borrowed much too often.
Her mother cried first, then bought herself some chocolate
and ate it all herself. On the red carpet by the reception desk
lay three giant lizards from Lee Kyung Ho.
The one with forks and knives in its jaws
snapped every time the receptionist spoke in Spanish.
She drooled red spittle. Her diapers leaked.
It was high time to buy herself an Afro-American doll.
To hang the miniature peasant shoes on the rearview mirror,
so that the shadows by the road could begin to walk in them too.
With her welfare check her mother had a skylight made over her cradle
so that when she got cramps she could thrust her hands into God.
When she was two her grandmother said to her:
"Child, God forbid you become a loafer while you still eat your mother's loaf."
When she was twenty she ate her mother roasted for New Year's Eve.
When she was three her grandfather said to her:
"Child, God forbid you have to go to a doctor
to have a human hand touch you."
When she was thirty she made an appointment for a Pap smear.
Her cousins washed their second-cousins' jeans
in the tub. And she couldn't swim.
She could only plunge and do crawl strokes in the village well

without realizing why Jesus loved her so much
that he saved her before the flood though they weren't close relatives,
or doctor and patient. The boys' cocks were falling,
cut off by the denying NO
that she kept in a box for beads.
The house defied the trailer on the other side of the fence.
She scrubbed her elbows with steel wool
and smooth as bronze started dancing a tango in the park
with the national hero from the last war.
Love happened suddenly, like Jesus's arrival on Earth.
For nine months she was a bottle with a champagne cork
that her husband couldn't open with his outsize fingers.
National heroes do not push perambulators, or cement barrows
or supermarket trolleys, or sledges, or mowers,
and a man who doesn't push some sort of cart cannot be head of the house.
Before giving birth, she broke a bottle over his head
and realized: one child of love is an additional ten square meters of
        ground space
and a war memorial one additional meter under the ground.
You get inflammation of the muscles
from raising your arms to God, and from caressing a statue too,
not only from photographing the Empire State Building.
And she gave birth, arms under head, stretched in a heavenly solarium,
because a cesarean is only for empresses giving birth under anesthesia,
so that the emperors are the first to see the baby,
a cesarean is a patriarchal inheritance,
the first cry is heard by the begetter, not the mother—
an intermediary between the Father and Son as well as the Holy Mother,
a living wall between the bronze husband and Sinai Hospital.
The baby's cry was an earthquake that made old ladies
with faces in Botox masks run out of the beauticians'
and women with their heads still under dryers from the hairdressers'
and children who had not yet grown their sixth teeth from the dentists'

and the dead without organs from operating theaters
and people without passwords from Internet cafés.
No one came back, only the national hero.
She was discharged from the maternity ward
on the third day, for the three Fates
to meet them behind the hotel door
with baseball bats and a gauge to measure the blood bronze content.
"An all-inclusive life awaits this baby," the maid whispered to her.
The TV channels sang "Heavenly Empress, Triumphant Empress"
and then for a full forty days
a gigantic man cast in bronze
stood in front of room no. 1012,
his muscles maddening the guests with passion
so that they made love in front of their children,
the father stood like a Jehovah's Witness before her
explaining, interpreting, and smilingly waiting
for the door to tire of banging, the keyhole of the key,
the peephole of curses as juicy as tomatoes,
for her heart to rise like pizza dough,
for love to froth like foam in a beer glass,
but in this world only national heroes have time
and ideal women full agendas,
umbilical cells in a bank and a Nobel laureate's book on the bedside table.
At that time she was just a woman giggling
at English humor and baby's finger
aiming like an arrow at the little bear on her pajamas,
like a red-hot rod digging in the bronze heart
the soul was melting the matter, the matter the soul.
"My right hand is itching," she would say to the baby,
and place it in the toaster and in two to three minutes her short story
was written in the parallel lines on her palm. The maids got bored
with the baby, cooee-coooeeing, goo-goo-gooing all the time,
the guests got tired, their lips dried from gaping,

wrinkled with smiling for a baby that never smiles,
just watches and listens and in it, like in a bottle on a tree,
the pear of life grows, fed by the juices,
distilling the self, waiting for the spring
to break out of the bottle, to become independent.
And it couldn't resist the whistle that leaped like a stone in the alcohol,
dived, jumped headfirst,
played ball, and swam naked
as the father grew ever smaller, and the mother ever bigger.
Between that time and this the little printed bears stand on the alert,
encouraging the child with its last efforts to send its mother off on
   a pilgrimage
in quest of fallen empires, and its father to the smelting plant,
it has canceled all the all-inclusive trips
and stretched out on its cot with a hard mattress for healthy sleep—
there it is, dreaming of overcooked macaroni melting in the mouth
a tongue that needs no translations
a world untapped by ancestors and descendants
and a life al dente, a life imperial, imperial.

Ars Poetica Ballad

To dig out what is live in my writing
do I have to bury those living in the world?
The worst of the dead are the best characters,
but when my gran says, "Child, don't put us in a book,
so folks won't laugh at us,"
I'm troubled by that angst of talent that gives birth to uniqueness
and my fingers go numb before my eyes
as if I were standing on a skyscraper
and everything appeared within my reach
but if I jump there won't be any mattress waiting for me.
I've got sisters rotting in prison
I've got brothers who can't leave the country
I've got aunts casting black-magic spells on me
and my contemporaries have renounced me in the press,
some people will only remember that they know me
on their way to the Last Judgment,
ex-lovers measure my every word precisely,
free and furious for being the same yet different,
children at school say I'm a dog trainer
until I end up in intensive care.
Behind every sexual organ hides a political move
every opened grave hides a family vault
and I'm drawn by that discord among those I feel close to
and those I feel distant from,
I'm haunted by my own DNA for it's carried by my children too,
I'm vexed by a story that I similarly vex.
And this ascetic life hides a gourmet's memories
of a basin painted with a violet
that I scalded my granddad's feet in,

of the room/aquarium where my uncle, shortsighted,
feeds smaller fish with big ones,
of the tango danced on the bean pods
with the man who went off with another man,
and how on Saturdays we used a Figaro trimmer to thin each other's hair,
and on Mondays we secretly opened the dead neighbor's bank statements.
Rather than the police I always called an ambulance,
rather than appealing for the banishment of death
I looked for the salvation of life,
but for the living life is not the same presence
as is death nonpresence for the dead.
Seated cross-legged in a Chicago airport
halfway through the closed season for hunting
halfway through the season for organic child conception
A. and I pass now a ball then a red card to each other.
It's a spring coiled between God's commandment and the breach of it,
and the more familiar the apostate the better we know its essence,
it bounces under the skin, returns below the bone.
As long as they're not put in a book
the faults and virtues of those who are close to us
are like the years-long barking of the neighbor's dog
or the tolling of church bells
at a precisely determined time:
they don't bother us as long as the neighbor
doesn't buy a new dog, or the church a digital loudspeaker;
then one takes leave of God
and God of animals and everyone slanders everyone else,
while I hold in the thought like a full bladder to the nearest loo
but outside I can no longer remember
whose initials I wear on the birch-bark brooch
or whether Rimbaud used the Charleville support hose
to gather the dreams of beans
soaked in water he would change seven times,

and none come to the surface.
Clerics attend a course in creative writing,
practice sermons passed through the eye of a needle.
"Hold out your hands," they say, but mine are hollow:
at the next service I'll sit between two empty seats
or between war veterans without arms or prostheses.
Kraków remembered Czeslaw's breath for thirty years,
but forgot his signature, his handwriting,
and every four months I enter Skopje
with a different suitcase,
fifty-two journeys like fifty-two cards for Black Peter
which I no longer know how to play.
I never returned dead from any of my travels,
I never set off alive on any of them,
but, just before I left,
my red portable cassette-player smashed my glasses
and since then the world's been a giant picture-book
where the dwarves become invisible.
I've got a private graveyard with fifty-two tombstones
bearing no historic epitaphs, pulling at my sleeve
to play hide-and-seek, it's a nice graveyard,
where the dead know only their mother tongue.
I've inherited from my dad the ulcers in my mouth
and from my mum, my gran.
I wore a white slip under a blue-trimmed skirt
when I first set foot in the house of my father's forebears.
Seated on three-legged stools they scratched their skin,
black and rough like unwatered soil round tomato plants.
"You're ours as much as the dirt under our nails," they said to me,
and I had to open my manicure set. My uncle retorted
with the story about the mouse in a pumpkin who became a boy.
It was a struggle between aesthetic achievements:
unreturned umbrellas from promotional packages,

a typewriter from a state-owned enterprise,
ashtrays from restaurants' summer terraces,
a dictionary of angels from the supermarket,
copper rings from a country fair.
Objects I can't recognize when they don't spend the night at home,
they lead a life of their own:
the suit at the dry cleaner's
and *Metamorphoses* at the bishop's,
and the ID in the drawer in the council offices,
and the house in the truck in the schoolyard,
and the life transferred to a book,
but what will become of them when they return home,
will they be the same or estranged,
will they be poetics or poetry?
I can only fulfill one destiny, but not my own,
I can only write one poem, but not mine.
Yet I've repented of everything, and everything has been returned to me,
and I've returned everything
except myself,
because to the One who forgives our debts
we owe much, much more
than our debtors owe us.

About the Author

Lidija Dimkovska was born in 1971 in Skopje, Macedonia. She attained a doctoral degree in Romanian poetry in Bucharest. She lives in Ljubljana, Slovenia, teaching world literature at the University of Nova Gorica and translating Slovenian and Romanian literature into Macedonian. In her native language she has published five books of poetry and one novel, and has edited an anthology of young Macedonian poets. In 2006 Ugly Duckling Presse in New York City published her first collection of poetry in English, *Do Not Awaken Them with Hammers.* Her books have been translated into German, Polish, Romanian, Bulgarian, Slovenian, and Slovakian. She has participated at numerous international literary readings and residencies, and has received many literary awards, including the award for the best debut book of poetry, for the best prose book of the year, and the European Hubert Burda award for poetry.

Since 1972, Copper Canyon Press has fostered the work of emerging, established, and world-renowned poets for an expanding audience. The Press thrives with the generous patronage of readers, writers, booksellers, librarians, teachers, students, and funders—everyone who shares the belief that poetry is vital to language and living.

MAJOR SUPPORT HAS BEEN PROVIDED BY:

THE PAUL G. ALLEN FAMILY FOUNDATION

Lannan

THE MAURER FAMILY FOUNDATION

NATIONAL ENDOWMENT FOR THE ARTS

WASHINGTON STATE ARTS COMMISSION

The Paul G. Allen Family Foundation
Amazon.com
Anonymous
Arcadia Fund
John Branch
Diana and Jay Broze
Beroz Ferrell & The Point, LLC
Mimi Gardner Gates
Carolyn and Robert Hedin
Golden Lasso, LLC
Gull Industries, Inc.
on behalf of William and Ruth True
Lannan Foundation
Rhoady and Jeanne Marie Lee
Maurer Family Foundation
National Endowment for the Arts
New Mexico Community Foundation
Penny and Jerry Peabody
Joseph C. Roberts
Cynthia Lovelace Sears and Frank Buxton
Washington State Arts Commission
Charles and Barbara Wright

bout underwriting Copper Canyon Press titles, please call 360-385-4925 ext. 103

The Chinese character for poetry is made
up of two parts: "word" and "temple." It also
serves as pressmark for Copper Canyon Press.

This book is set in Parable, designed by Christopher
Burke. Heads are set in Stone Informal, designed by
Sumner Stone. Book design and composition by
Valerie Brewster, Scribe Typography. Printed on
archival-quality paper at McNaughton & Gunn, Inc.